This book belongs to:

An Amazing Person!

Text Copyright © 2015 Jessie Shepherd

Illustrations Copyright © 2015 Tyler Shepherd

All rights reserved. This book or any portion thereof may not be reproduced or used in any manner whatsoever without the express written permission of the publisher except for the use of brief quotations in a book review.

First Printing, 2015

ISBN 978-1-943880-11-9

Library of Congress Control Number 2015947216

BlueFox Press

Salt Lake City, UT 84121

BlueFoxPress.com

Gordy the Rabbit has ADHD

by jessie shepherd, ACMHC   illustrations ty shepherd

an imprint of
BlueFox Press

This is Gordy.

He has Attention-Deficit/
Hyperactivity Disorder.

ADHD for short.

Gordy has a hard time focusing on one thing at a time.

Sometimes he wiggles and squirms in his seat.
He just feels restless.

Gordy has a difficult time at school.

Some of the kids bully him and call him names.

People get frustrated with him because he will start a task and get sidetracked.

Sometimes he is late to places.

He forgets important items like his wallet, glasses or even a pencil.

Some people think of Gordy as lazy and messy.

Gordy can seem rude.

He forgets to ask permission to use other people's belongings.

He also runs and climbs on things that you should not run or climb on.

Gordy has a hard time waiting his turn.

He can't help but blurt out the answers.

He gets so excited.

But Gordy can learn skills so he can get tasks done and still do what he enjoys.

Making lists and planning ahead can help with remembering.

If Gordy has a routine, he doesn't get confused and knows what is expected of him.

Having Attention Deficit/Hyperactivity Disorder has some incredible parts too.

Gordy has a ton of energy.

Which makes it so he can get a lot done in a day and still be ready for fun.

His curiosity can lead him on many exciting adventures.

He can see answers to problems that others might have missed.

Gordy can pay attention to all the details large and small.

This lets him see the big picture.

People with ADHD are very enthusiastic.

They can get others excited about something great they have discovered.

They pick up careers that they are very interested in.

This makes them very successful.

Gordy is also courageous because he follows his heart, making the possibilities endless!

Best way to interact with someone with ADHD

-Structure is key to creating good habits and reducing negative behaviors.

-Be patient. They are not misbehaving just to frustrate you.

-Limit distractions if you are looking for them to pay attention.

-Do physical activity. Playing sports, exercise and dancing are all ways to get some of that energy out.

-Give them unstructured time. They should have downtime where they do not have to focus.

-Seek professional support for you and your family. Behavioral Therapy has great success in treatment of ADHD. Medication may also be an option to discuss with your health care provider.

www.ingramcontent.com/pod-product-compliance
Lightning Source LLC
Chambersburg PA
CBHW051248110526
44588CB00025B/2925